CW01262517

Auchterarder
in old picture postcards volume 2

by Joan Macintosh

European Library ZALTBOMMEL/THE NETHERLANDS

GB ISBN 90 288 6318 4

© 1996 European Library – Zaltbommel/The Netherlands

No part of this book may be reproduced in any form, by print, photoprint, microfilm or any other means, without written permission from the publisher.

Introduction

The coat of arms of Auchterarder shows high rocks and hills, a castle, falcons – *A city set on a hill cannot be hid* says the motto. The hill is based on hard volcanic rocks and deposits of glacial origin formed 350 million years ago. Iron Age men made camp here and Picts and Romans in their time disputed the strategically placed valley of Strathearn.

Auchterarder lies halfway between Perth and Stirling, cities of critical importance in Scottish history: Stirling guarding the passes to the Highlands and Perth with its ancient royal palace of Scone, where Scottish kings were crowned.

Central to these power points, Auchterarder contained the hunting lodge of Malcolm Canmore, King of the Scots in the 11th century – a halting place between battles for Edward I of England and Robert Bruce. The Queen Regent, mother of Mary Queen of Scots, signed here, reluctantly, the 1559 Treaty of Auchterarder, officially recognising Protestantism in Scotland. In 1715 the town, like others in the path of Charles Stuart's retreating supporters, suffered total destruction in the famous 'Burning'. Yet by the year 1800 new houses – plain but practical – replaced those destroyed along the mile long High Street of 'The Lang Toon'.

This book deals with more settled times – the century before the Second World War. It was not a large parish – between 1836 and 1931 the population hovered around 3,000-3,500 – modestly prosperous. Farming was expanding on a scale not possible in the narrow strips of the old crofts. Weaving became a prosperous industry. The title of 'Royal Burgh' lapsed, but not the strong local pride.

Distinguished old families in the area – Grahams, Haldanes, Drummonds – were joined by wealthy entrepreneurs – Reids, Hallys, Whites. However, the character of the place was most striking in its independent-minded townsfolk. Dramatic evidence of this lies in its turbulent church history. Mediaeval Celtic saints – whose chapels sleep in surrounding woodlands – were succeeded by centuries of theological debate – the 1559 Treaty, the 1717 Auchterarder Creed, successive Secessions in the 18th century, the 1843 Disruption – doctrinal issues which wracked churchmen and laymen. At the centre of these debates was Auchterarder. This was no mean place!

Joan Macintosh

Footnote: For those who find Auchterarder's name difficult to spell or pronounce – take heart… it used to be worse!: Outreard and Oughtrerdorer (1296); Uthrardor (1305); Uchtirardour (1581); Ochterairder (1596); Uachdarard- or the Gaelic, Uachdar Ardhobar… all meaning 'the summit of the rising ground'.

This book supplements an earlier book in the series about Auchterarder during the same period. It is not a history book – but postcards and photographs help to bring history to life by illustrating what people valued in their lives at that time. Several poems in the Auchterarder Local History Association records have been quoted. One leaflet circa 1890 'Auchterarder Past and Present: By a Native after a long absence: Price two-pence; Tovani & Co. Auchterarder': believed to have been by George Oswald. Andrew Deuchars, also quoted, was another popular Auchterarder bard.

Also much used were the Statistical Parish Records of 1844; *From One Century to Another: reminiscences of Miss Elizabeth Haldane of Cloan*, published in 1937 by Alex. Maclehose & Co.; *The Annals of Auchterarder and Memorials of Strathearn* by A.G. Reid.

Many thanks for help and advice are owing to – amongst many others – Kenneth Young W.S., Martha Soutar, Moira Cowie and Marjorie Ross of the A.L.H.A., Dr. James Grant, Mr. and Mrs. Ian Hally, Mr. and Mrs. R. Haldane, Nigel Clarke.

1 Craigrossie.

If seeking Auchterarder, look along the horizon of the Ochil Hills for the characteristic humpbacked shape of Craig Rossie. The Craig is not exceptionally high – 1,349 feet – but it dominates the strath. The view from the peak is extensive – westwards to Argyll's Cruach nan Capull (2,005 feet) 56 miles away and Ben Lomond (3,192 feet) 38 miles; northwards, Ben Macdhui (4,296 feet), highest peak in the Cairngorms, 53 miles; eastwards, the River Tay to Dundee and, on a clear day, the Tay Bridge. The view of rich farmlands is less forested than when the Picts in their upland forts watched Romans marching below in the first centuries of this millenium. A fairly gentle climb leads to this great vista of abiding history. Auchterarder itself lies in the strath on its own low hill, beside Ruthven water at the foot of Craig Rossie.

HEUGH O' COUL AND CRAIGROSSIE, AUCHTERARDER

2 Auchterarder – 1860.

Look north in 1860 from the Ochil Hills towards the Lang Toon. Sheep still grazed in the South Crofts, where soon there would be mills and houses for mill workers. Outstanding buildings, from west to east, were Belvidere (1849), home of William Young, Bank Agent and Solicitor (p.19); the Relief Church with its four corner spires, built by schismatic congregations (p.20); the Free Church, later St. Andrew's, built in 1849, after the Disruption (p.18) and another 'Secession Church', originally from Kinkell – three churches inspired by congregational doctrinal differences of opinion.

AUCHTERARDER,
From the South
Published by James Martin, 21 Greenside St. Edinburgh

3 Aytoun Hall at the Cross.

The mile-long High Street, with narrow wynds (lanes) but few side streets, formed the 'Lang Toon'. Half way, at the Cross, the Town Hall, opened in 1872 by the Laird of Ochtertyre, Sir Patrick Murray, was gratefully named after Captain Aytoun of Glen Devon, who in 1833 had engineered the town's water supply from Crook o' Moss in the Ochils. Here the town's great occasions were held – charity bazaars, balls, official celebrations. The fine fountain in this 1872 drawing was removed in 1905, being inconvenient for new traffic. A drinking fountain set in the wall celebrated new water supplies for the growing town from Duchally Glen. Beside the Hall Girnal House, built in 1790 as a grain store, was now the Institute. Then comes the Masonic Temple, a powerful influence in the town.

THE AYTOUN HALL   AUCHTERARDER

4   The Institute.

The Institute – across the road from these boys – was the place for magic lantern shows for the boys, and lectures and classes for serious-minded townsfolk. In the 1880s the Haldanes of Cloan promoted well-attended lectures (1/6 a season) on subjects like 'Health' – illustrated by a skeleton and stomach pump – and the Theory of Relativity (Einstein was a good friend). Lighter entertainments were a billiard room (entry 1p.)– the Cyclists' Rest tea room – dominos and chess – a famous choir – a public library and reading room. A fairly typical reader was a ploughman working his way through three volumes of Schopenhauer. However, church elders were said to check surreptitiously what the pernicious novels of George Eliot – reputed atheist – were like. The Institute also provided '*Hot and Cold Baths@ 9p.* (bring your own towel)'. Baths in High Street homes – if any – were portable tubs without running water.

5 Ladies' Bazaars

Ladies' Bazaars were enormously popular in the new Aytoun Hall. The 1873 bazaar cleared the last penny of the £3,000 which the building cost, complete with imposing tower, hall with balcony and fine panelling in the Council Chamber. Everyone came. (Is that Provost Hally's hat and smile in the centre?) (p.52). An 1844 commentator wrote cautiously: *The people are in general much disposed to industry… economical… yet in general by no means disinclined to humane and charitable actions.* In the 1920s the balcony was popular with children, who could watch their elders dancing to the latest jazz tunes.

6 Masonry.

The Masonic Hall at the Cross in Auchterarder is central to the Lodge of St. John No. 46 Charter dating from the historic year of 1745. Their most treasured possession, presented in 1792, is this huge two-handled sword of Sir John de Graeme, carried by him at the Battle of Falkirk in 1298, where he was killed and his good friend William Wallace defeated by Edward I. In 1910 the Tyler of the Lodge bears the sword at the Lodge door. Masonry was a powerful influence in the town, most leading citizens being members. Aytoun Hall's opening in 1872 was virtually a Masonic ceremony. In 1859 Worshipful Master George Hally opened the Masonic Hall to the townsfolk for all-night celebrations of Rabbie Burns' centenary – dancing, marches, songs and a rumbustious presentation of Tam o' Shanter.

7 High Street.

In the early 1900s the High Street was a pleasant place for boys to play – even at night, illuminated by gas light, sufficient, they said, *to make the darkness visible*. The old stone slab 'bridges' – *brigs at ilka door*, boasted the local poet – crossed the dirty water in roadside gullies. In 1906 water was still drawn from roadside pumps. At the corner of Montrose Road is the handsome gable end of the draper's shop originally built by local mill owner William Hally (p.52), as an outlet for his textiles. His initials, carved above the door, served later for young Watson Hogg – 'Bertie' Hogg – enterprising ex-grocer's apprentice, who once sold his wares round the county from a pony cart like the one in the picture.

High Street, Auchterarder.

29th September

8 Star Hotel and the Post Office.

Near Aytoun Hall stands the Star Hotel – 'oldest established hotel in the district' – a regular halt for coaches and post horses. In 1905, still advertising 'Carriages and Horses', it added proudly, 'MOTOR CAR FOR HIRE' and a local telephone number – No. 7. The Misses Carmichael, proprietresses, endured the bleak period in 1920-1923 when Auchterarder led other Scottish towns going 'dry' under the 'Local Veto'. The town's 21 public houses (for a population of approximately 3,000) suffered, as customers made long journeys to non-dry towns, disregarding children in The Band of Hope (p.63) with banners saying: *Wha would hae a drunken man?* There was markedly less drunkeness in the streets; but finally the Veto was voted out. Next door is the 1905 Post Office. In 1837, when Victoria became Queen, one elderly lady, Mrs. Stewart, did all the work of receiving, sorting, forwarding and delivering local mail. By 1897 a staff of 15 made three deliveries a day in town. By 1905 the level of work required a new office, replacing two houses.

9 No. 101 High Street

No. 101, High Street in 1922 had belonged for four centuries to the same family – shoemakers, joiners, cabinet makers – Graemes, Drummonds and Moirs by name. The passage leads through to the garden and croft land behind. Two families lived in the house and a downstairs room was let to a potato merchant and used as Liberal Party Election Room when required. Two rooms upstairs were let to a father and two daughters. The owners kept four rooms for themselves. Perceptions of adequate living space were not the same as now. People slept, lived and ate in the same room. Most houses in the street would have been equally or more packed, with three or four families and eight or ten children normal.

10   Inside No. 101 High Street.

It is unusual to see inside a typical town house of 1919. On the right, in the front living room, is the cooking range – handsome kettle always on the hob; candlesticks and family treasures on the mantlepiece; a three legged stool for youngsters by the sofa corner where Granddad always sat. All the furniture was made by him – a cabinet maker. On the left is the curtained cupboard bed, built into the massive stone wall, used by as many children as required. The big cupboard was packed with table and bed linen and family goods. There is a glimpse through to the back room which, with two upstairs rooms, provided living space for a family of four or five – or more.

11 Behind 101 High Street.

Behind No. 101 a small back garden is all that is left of the long narrow croft which once stretched northwards (p.12).

There's a wee, wee plot o' garden ground / At oor back door. / A bonnier spot could not be found / Than oor back door. / There's a railing roond about / And a gate to let you out / And an apple tree wi' fruit on't / At oor back door.

The ladies of the house – Mrs. Isabella Moir McGilp with daughter and friend – are admiring the fruit bushes. Over the hedge is a line of washing and the gable end of the Misses Carmichael's Laundry which served the town's housewives. White blouses, shirts and long skirts needed a lot of washing; even housewives who laundered at home might use the Laundry mangle. The gable end on the right is the old Secession Church, used as a cattle mart when the church moved to Montrose Road.

12 Airview of Auchterarder, 1933.

This postcard of the town in 1933 caught the last clear glimpse of the original crofts, north and south of the street. These sharply defined strips of property traditionally provided the arable farming land of the township, surviving from the days when most townsfolk were part-time farmers. Some crofts have become back gardens, but long fields still reach into the farm lands. The Bowling Club (p.69) stands out.

13 The Feus.

When the Barony of Auchterarder was forfeited in the 18th century by James Drummond, Jacobite Earl of Perth, sections of his land – 'feus' – were sold, from Hunter Street northwards. The Auchterarder Feus were always a close-knit community – not rich, but (with exceptions) thoroughly respectable. Everyone knew everyone. Eighty years on an old man who had been a child there could recite the relationships and life histories of everyone who lived in the Feus from one end to another. Between some houses narrow wynds led to weaving sheds, cow byres, pig stys, drying greens and gardens. Back there, chatting across fences, life was really lived, rather than in the street.

14 Four generations in the Feus.

In 1911 four generations of the Dunn family (John, James, John, James) are in the back garden of their Feus house. Great-Grandfather was born in 1829. Masons, plumbers, weavers – the men are manifest pillars of this community. In their church going suits they look the camera straight in the eye – as they would face any man. The gardens of these houses were for use, not ornament – more potatoes than roses.

15   Schoolgirls.

1904 – and girls at Auchterarder School are growing up – wearing their very best clothes for the class photograph. The fine lace of many collars was probably the work of mothers and grandmothers skilled in the craft. In ten years, these girls would be ready for or already embarked upon marriage to local boys. Then there would come motherhood of children who would follow the pattern of their own lives. Many of them and their husbands would work locally in the mills, farms, shops or clerical jobs. However, that predictable routine of life was due for upheaval. In ten years they would find themselves part of 'The Great War' – as it was called until an even greater one came along.

16 Hunter Street.

Unlike the plain houses of the Feus were the grander homes in this 1914 picture of Hunter Street. It ran north from the Police Station past Auchterarder House (p.40) to Innerpeffray, Kinkell Church, Crieff – a route through hundreds of years of history. Now it was tarred for motor traffic, with garage services from the Coach Works, previously a stables providing a pony trap to the Railway Station. Photography was new enough in 1914 for children to run out from their homes and pose hopefully for a picture. In the evening they would be watching the lamplighters – Sandy Smeaton or Tom Riddoch – lighting the gaslamps with long flame-tipped poles.

17 Western Road.

At the other end of the town is this corner of Orchil and Western Roads. A townsman brings his sheep home from grazing on the Common Muir (p.29) to the byre down the wynd behind his Feus home. Changes are taking place in this rural scene about 1920. Western Road's high hedges are for the privacy of wealthy incomers from Glasgow, building holiday homes – their 'villas' – in Auchterarder, where they can enjoy golf, shooting, fishing and other rural pleasures – and retire in due course. Better rail and road communication began to make commuting possible. Improved water supplies from Duchally Glen (p.31) encouraged building, with modern drainage, at this end of Auchterarder.

18 Coul.

Coul, the home of the Burgh Smeatons and once part of the Marquis of Montrose's estate, is typical of the style of house dotting the Ochils from the early 18th century onwards. Rather grander than most, it reflects the unostentatious domestic style that well to do landowners enjoyed – surrounded by good shooting and fishing as well as productive farming and woodland. Nearby Heugh o' Coul (p.30) was a well-loved beauty spot on the estate.

19 The Lairds.

The landowners were as close a community as the townsfolk. Patrick Burgh Smeaton, born in 1833, was last of six generations of Smitton or Smeaton who lived near or at Coul, lying on the Ochil Hills below Craig Rossie. He is with his wife, Margaret Young, daughter of the local Writer (i.e. solicitor) and Bank Agent, who had the fine house of Belvidere (p.2). Their only child was a daughter who married a Smeaton cousin to keep the estate together; but eventually financial difficulties prevailed and they emigrated to Canada.

Not an unusual solution to money problems in the late 19th century.

20   The old parish church.

The old parish church was the 1660 Presbyterian successor of the pre-Reformation church at Kirkton down Hunter Street. It had an eventful history, including a riot in 1712 when the congregation objected to an English-style funeral as 'popery'. Rebuilt in 1764 with stones from the Grahams' attainted and demolished Kincardine Castle, it was extended in 1811 to accommodate 930 'sittings' from a population of about 2,500. Most famous was its role as the scene of the 1843 Disruption debate (p.21). *Aye mony a teuch debate was there / At the disruption time.* It was demolished in the early 20th century, except for its tower.

21   Inside old parish church.

This rare 1905 picture shows the interior of the old parish church shortly before demolition. The central pulpit for the Minister, with a seat for the Precentor at a lower level, was characteristic of the reformed churches. Here the fierce debates took place culminating in the Disruption. The Westminster Patronage Act had denied the congregation's right to overturn the choice of new Minister by the local patron – the Earl of Kinnoull. Auchterarder – famous for its stubborn defense of congregational rights – eventually took its case to the House of Lords. The Lords found against them, but the dissenters were not to be put down. They seceded – and set up a new church. There were lions in the churches in those days!

INTERIOR OF PARISH CHURCH, AUCHTERARDER.

22 The Relief Church.

Congregations seceding on doctrinal issues from the parish churches in Blackford and Auchterarder, joined in a Relief Church — *relief for Christians oppressed in their Christian privilege.* They held services in open fields until in 1780 a church was built for 583 members near the Tent Ground, a field in which they still held occasional outdoor services. The building took six months, by… *their own unaided labours after the ordinary day's toil was over,* at a cost of £800. Some 130 seceders emigrated in the 1830s to settle with fellow Presbyterians in the mountains of upper New York State. Those who stayed home joined forces eventually with another Secession Church which moved from Kinkell via Star Wynd to Montrose Road. Wherever they worshipped the church was central to their lives: *There's a kirk within a yard or two at oor back door / Where they preach the terrors o' the Law at oor back door. / Ye can hear the organ play sacred hymns and psalmody… at oor back door.* (A. Deuchars circa 1902.)

23 The Rev. George Jacque.

In 1835 the young Rev. George Jacque answered a call from the Relief Church in Auchterarder. He ministered here for 57 years. Every account of him is admiring and affectionate: *Golden tongued preacher... tall... well set up with a gentle way that no sinner could withstand...* He always wore the clerical long black coat and hat – walked everywhere, especially in the hills, to visit parishioners and to practice his sermons aloud amongst the sheep. His deep love of music at first horrified stern Secessioners. A delegation called to protest at his playing the cello – but were converted: *... nane o' thae squeakin feedles, but a muckle sounding, deep releegious feedle that played the Psalms of David.* The church became famous for its choir and the Minister even led off the Grand March at village dances.

24 Music they sang.

Music was mostly home-made in Auchterarder in this century. There was no shortage of local talent. A keen Institute Choir often represented Auchterarder in Scottish concerts and once in the Albert Hall in London. On this occasion, purely for local pleasure, South United Presbyterian Church— previously the Relief Church — was singing under the chairmanship of the Reverend George Jacque. The songs they sang were, far from the Psalms of David, a wealth of sentimental and lyrical favourites... "*Our Concerts were aye filled t'door / No even room to move / Many a canty nicht was spent / Lang syne in Masons' Lodge*' (Tovani v.11.) Later concerts were held in the fine new Aytoun Hall.

CONCERT.

THE SOUTH U. P. CHURCH CHOIR

will give their Second ANNUAL CONCERT, under the Leadership of their Conductor Mr JOHN DUNN, in the

AYTOUN HALL,

ON THE EVENING OF

WEDNESDAY, 18TH APRIL.

Rev. Mr Jacque, in the Chair.

PROGRAMME—PART FIRST.

Glee,	Hark Apollo,	Choir.
Song,	Norah the pride of Kildare,	Mr P. Mailer.
Duet,	Damon and Clora,	Miss I. Sanderson & Mr J. Anderson.
Part Song,	I'm ower young to marry yet,	Choir.
Song,	John Brown,	Mr James Dunn.
Part Song,	The Campbells are coming,	Choir.
Trio	Bridal Bells,	Ladies.
Song,	Barney,	Mr James Anderson.
Part Song,	Highland Watch,	Choir.
Duet,	All's Well,	Messrs Jas. Dunn & P. Mailer.
Part Song,	The Norse National Song,	Choir.

PART SECOND.

Part Song,	Happy we've been a' th'gether,	Choir.
Song,	The women are a' gane wud,	Mr P. Mailer.
Trio,	Chimney Sweepers Glee,	Messrs Dunn, Anderson, & P. Mailer.
Duet,	Ye needna be courtin' at me auld man,	Miss H. Morrison & Mr John Dunn.
Song		Mr James Anderson.
Glee,	Rosabelle,	Choir.
Song,	Be kind to auld Grannie,	Mr Jas. Dunn.
Glee,	Æolian Lyre,	Choir.
Duet,	A. B. C.	Miss S. Dunn & Mr P. Mailer.
Song,	Grannie's Leather Pouch,	Mr P. Mailer.
Chorus,	Call John, (by request.)	Choir.

Doors open at half-past 7. Chair to be taken at 8 o'clock.

Tickets may be had from Messrs P. Faichney, Jos. Hepburn, Jas. Fisher, P. Anderson, Mrs. Miller, and Members of Choir.

ADMISSION—Front Seats, 1s ; Back Seats, 6d.

25   Cloan in 1869.

Around Auchterarder lie the great houses of families which for generations held this valuable and strategically situated land. The Haldanes, in Glen Eagles since the early middle ages, were amongst the more intellectually distinguished – philosophers, scientists, statesmen. Their family home and chapel remained in the Glen, but branches spread to other houses in the Ochils – Foswell, Airthry Castle and Cloan. Cloan was a simple farmhouse until 1865 when transformed, according to current fashion, into spectacular Scottish Baronial style. The family played a benign role in the town which Cloan overlooked – supporting every kind of local good works – influencing, but not intervening in, civic affairs (p.4).

26   Miss Elizabeth Haldane spinning.

Characteristic of intellectually inclined Haldanes was Miss Elizabeth Haldane C.H. (1862-1937). While other ladies embroidered she practised local crafts – carding, spinning and weaving wool. As a girl she could not share university life with her brilliant brothers, yet she translated the philosophical works of Descartes and Hegel – still recommended texts for students. Practical and energetic, she helped to found the British Red Cross and was concerned with all Auchterarder interests. Cloan kept open house for distinguished statesmen and scholars like Asquith, Churchill, Einstein – and also for local good causes. As Secretary of the new Library she solicited donations from her friend Andrew Carnegie and organised lectures on subjects like explosives and philosophy.

27 The road to Cloan.

Cloan lay high in the Ochils at the end of a two mile road, familiar to townsfolk going to work or Sunday picnics, for walks across the hills – or meeting friends. *Noo the balmy breath of summer gently stirs the leafy trees / Gowans and yellow cowslips bespangle a' the leas / As I gang to meet wi' Lizzie who I brawly well dae ken / Will be waiting on my coming at the brig below Cloanden.* (A. Deuchars 1887.) Compared with other customary walks – Blackford (4 H miles), Dunning (5 miles), Muthill (6 miles) – it was no great distance, although the climb was steep. Behind the great house was a favourite swimming hole – a 'dookin' den' – by a small dam which, under the eminent supervision of Lord Kelvin, produced for Cloan the first domestic electricity in the county.

28 The funeral of Viscount Haldane of Cloan.

In August 1928, down that road from Cloan – past the mills up Abbey Road (p.50) down the long High Street, past Aytoun Hall (p.3) and on to the family chapel in Glen Eagles (p.35) – marched the funeral cortege of Viscount Lord Haldane, former Lord Chancellor, wartime Secretary of State for War, founder of the Territorial Army – philosopher and statesman. Lord Lucan represented the King. A macabre incident disturbed the solemnity. A man in morning suit tried to stop the procession, insisting the Viscount was not dead. He was firmly removed. That night he went to the family burial ground, dug up and opened the coffin – and found he was wrong! A shepherd driving his flock up the Glen early next morning found him weeping by the open coffin.

The Police Sergeant, summoned on his bicycle, put the Viscount respectfully back in his coffin and walked the culprit back to the Police Station for a sleep in the cells. There was no publicity…

29 The Common Muir.

Auchterarder's Common Muir 200 acres were for fifty years subject to bitter legal battle. In 1808... *from time immemorial everyone living in Auchterarder having a cow... had grazing rights as well as rights to quarry stones and cut turf... without leave asked or obtained from any.* New houses after the 1715 Burning were built of stone freely taken from the muir quarry. Then the Hon. Basil Cochran 'late of the East India Company' purchased the Barony and disputed these rights, claiming ownership. Auchterarder's townspeople would not submit, quoting a popular verse: *"The law doth punish man of woman / Who steals the goose from off the common. / Who sets the greater felon loose / Who steals the common from the goose?* It took fifty years for the Burgh to win an Act of Parliament (1860) vesting the Muir in their elected Commissioners. *The moor was then oor Public Park / Whaur we could jump and run / And we had aye a Public Bath / Doon at the Lochy Linn.* An annual cattle market was held here, but eventually the common good was found to lie in a fine golf course.

30 Heugh o' Coul.

*She does not love me any more...
and sadly, finally,... I DO NOT!*

The glory of Auchterarder lies in the hills — *I shall lift up mine eyes to the hills* — with its glens, rivers, waterfalls. In 1837 Heuch o' Coul was fairly described as a 'very stiking chasm' with its double waterfall under rocky banks. A shelter here, called a 'Fug Hoose', provided refuge for climbers when fog or snow suddenly descended. Like another 'fug hoose' near Cloan (p.27) it was simply built, but at one time furnished with cups, saucers and tea-making equipment. 'Fug hooses' were very popular, it was said, with courting couples wanting privacy. Some visits were recorded on the walls e.g.: *ED loves JC* ...

31 Duchally Glen inspection.

Captain Aytoun's original Crook o' Moss water supply (p.3) became inadequate as the town grew. In the new century a new source was tapped in Duchally Glen, providing enough for the Mills and new houses. The Town Council turned out in force each year to inspect the springs. In 1939 here were Provost Martin, Town Clerk Ross, Baillie Mitchell, Mr. R.M. Young, Town Clerk; Mr. Garrie, printer; Mr. Lambie, Loanhead farmer and Gordon Lockhart, Gleneagles golf professional. They dressed more for an official function than a hill climb, but carried a small basket for refreshment. Mr. Thomson, Burgh Surveyor, was an essential officer. It was long remembered how, on a winter inspection when pipes had frozen, he sank so deep in the snow that only his cap showed where he could be found and rescued.

32 Picnics.

In summertime everyone went on picnics – hills and burns providing much loved places. Food was often elaborate – sent ahead, to be ready when the party arrived with a healthy appetite. 'Fug hooses' (p.30) were sometimes near at hand if the weather turned nasty. Picnics brought men and women together. They were great opportunities to slip away from the crowd and talk more intimately. So everyone tried to look their best: sensible shoes, of course, but hats, fine blouses and skirts for the ladies; caps, ties and jackets for the gentlemen. Informality, as we know it, was inadmissible.

33 Kinkell Bridge.

Kinkell Bridge crosses the River Earn on the road to Crieff, near the ancient church dedicated to Celtic St. Bean in a Parish notorious for a 17th century scandal: *Was there e'er sic a parish, a parish, a parish / Was there e'er sic a parish as that o' Kinkell? / They've hangit the Minister, Drowned the precentor / Dang doon the steeple and drucken the bell*'. All broadly true – but it's a long story!

In later years this was a more tranquil place, easy walking distance from Auchterarder and famous for fishing. Salmon were plentiful, but trout fishing was 'the working man's recreation', not being protected for landlords by the law. An angler might see kingfishers, wagtails, herons, otters. He was certain to take home a good catch.

34 Curling at Kinkell.

In winter, below Kinkell Bridge, solid ice attracts the curlers. *The ponds are bearing!* was a call that would ring through the town. There was room for several rinks on this broad stretch of the Earn – and for ladies in warm winter dresses to stroll confidently. Summer Sunday afternoons saw quite a different scene here. Families walked out from the town with their prams, kettles and picnic baskets for a swim and leisurely refreshment.

35 Glen Eagles.

The road south from Auchterarder by the Ochil Hills, lies through deep and narrow Glen Eagles and Glen Devon. Here was the Drovers' Road along which for centuries highland cattle were driven to the Falkirk tryst. At the northern end of Glen Eagles are the ruins of the Castle, the 12th century chapel and Haldane burial place and the pleasant house, still home to the Haldanes, seen here in the distance. Coming northwards down the precipitous glen, travellers can see the distant lights of Crieff and beyond that the solid phalanx of the Grampian Hills, precisely as Roman armies and home-bound drovers would in their various times have seen them.

36 Tormaukin Inn, Glen Devon.

Every Drover's Road needs inns for refreshment. In Glen Devon drovers and travellers found old Tormaukin Inn on the sheltered side of the Glen, before entering narrow Glen Eagles. In the early 1920s motor transport has arrived with this old 'flivver'. Pony traps were still used and even more common transport through the glen is the bicycle. Two cyclists stand to admire the car – and the photographer. Looking north beyond them, from a high point of 900 feet, travellers will find the winding vista of Glen Eagles… gateway to Strathearn, to Auchterarder and to the north.

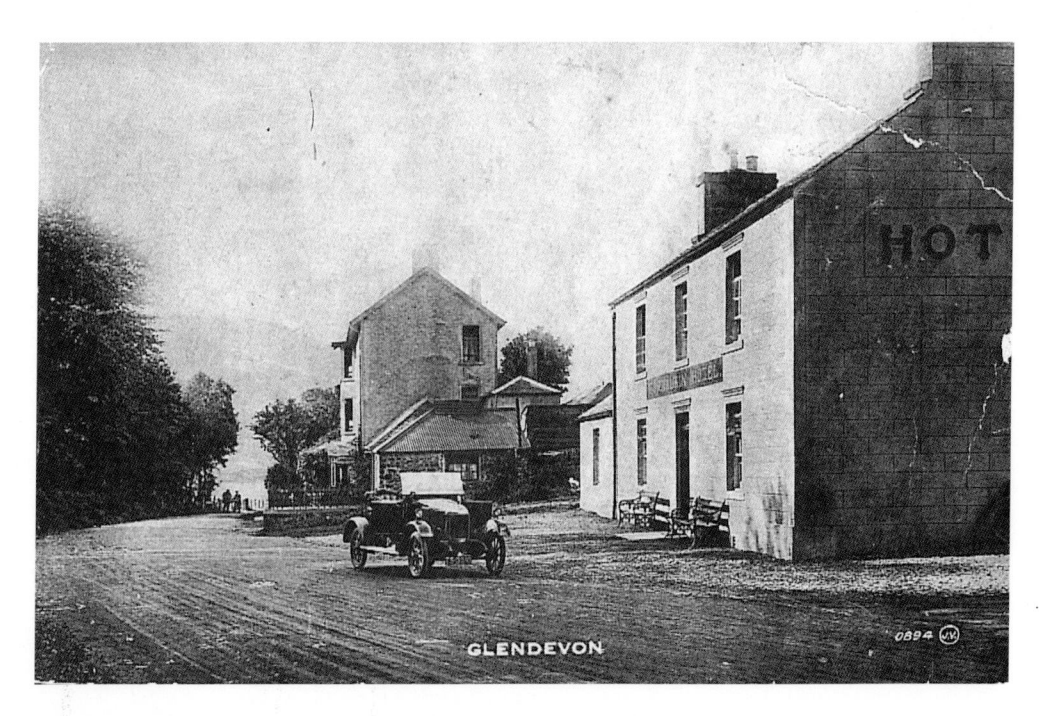

37 Aberuthven.

A good mile north of Auchterarder lies the village of Aberuthven. Until the early 19th century it was Smiddyhaugh – a blacksmith's forge by the bridge over the Ruthven – a convenient halt for travellers. The inn still survives. In the 19th century the village became a hive of home weavers. In 1919, when this picture was taken, weaving skills still survived, but they were mostly employed in the Auchterarder textile mills (p.50), to which 'the hands' trudged several miles every day, whatever the weather.

38 St. Kattans Church – Montrose Mausoleum.

Aberuthven was Graham country, the demesne of the Montrose family of Kincardine Castle. St. Kattans, an ancient Celtic chapel, was unused as a church after 1697, but sheltered the Montrose Mausoleum – *an elegant and chaste piece of architecture* by William Adam. The great Marquis himself, after dramatic turns of fortune, was not buried here, being executed in Edinburgh in 1658, as a supporter of Charles I. In the 1830s *a vulgar scene* marred the funeral of the recently deceased Duke. His opposition to the 1832 Reform Act, aimed at broadening the electorate, was resented by democratically inclined townsfolk. Rude remarks were shouted as the cortege passed – stones thrown. Violence in such a place of peace may seem inappropriate: yet it is worth observing loopholes through the churchyard walls, pierced by local Home Guards in the Second World War to enable them to repel the threat of advancing Germans! But they never came...

39 Auld Hoose o' Gask.

Most affectionately admired of local great houses is the Auld Hoose o' Gask, home of Carolina. Lady Nairn, the aristocratic Jacobite lady whose poems and songs – long attributed to Burns and Scott – include 'Charlie is my Darling', 'Will ye no come back again? 'The Hundred Pipers'.

Oh, the auld house, the auld house,
What tho' the rooms were wee;
O kind hearts were dwelling there
And bairnies fu' o' glee…
Oh, the auld laird, the auld laird,
Sae canty, kind and crouse,
How mony did he welcome to
His ain wee dear auld house.
And the leddy too, sae genty

There sheltered Scotland's heir
And clipt a lock wi' her ain hand
Frae his lang yellow hair.

40 Auchterarder House: The Reid family.

Amongst Auchterarder benefactors were the Reid family of Auchterarder House. James Reid made his fortune in Glasgow between 1847 and 1894, building up the great North British Company which manufactured locomotives for the world. He bought Auchterarder House from the long-established Hunter family, who had built it in such style that in 1844 it was described as 'the principal mansion in the Parish'. The Reids made more improvements, raising pedigree cattle and a famous garden. James Reid was a passionate golfer and is said to have died 'after a valiant but vain effort to play his ball from a difficult lie in a bunker'. His son, the Episcopalian Bishop of St. Andrew's, Dunkeld and Dunblane, built St. Kessog's Church as a memorial to his parents. The family also built, for the great benefit of the town, the fine cottage hospital, St. Margaret's.

41 Stooks at Castleton.

This familiar scene before the war is hardly remembered now – stooking the hay. Every available woman, child and outside labour lent a hand. The men scythed the hay, leaving it to be gathered in stooks, then carried in wagons to the farmyard, the hay was stacked by skilled workers. But times were changing. Across this field in Castleton – inconspicuous amongst the cottages – is a glimpse of William Hally's first small mill, where he started in 1863 to collect home weavers' work for sale in Glasgow. Then Hally installed power-driven looms – two at first, but 150 by 1869. There was work for all – children half-time, one day on the mill, the next at school 2/6 a week. In 1872 the mills moved to Ruthvendale (p.50), but the transformation of Auchterarder began in Castleton.

42 Haystacks.

A sight almost vanished from our landscape – this noble display of haystacks in 1906 was the work of some of the most valuable men on the farm. Not everyone could master the art. There was much satisfaction – not only for the farmer at Millhaugh – as the year's bounty was gathered in. Although the ground was rich, its volcanic origin had over centuries required arduous improvement. In 1844 an observer wrote: *Boulders were of very frequent occurrence… but by aid of gunpowder… they had mostly been forced to quit the field and take their place in the fence.* Thence the universal dry stone dykes (uncemented walls) (p.48).

Millhaugh and Ochil Hills, Dunning

43   Farming – Milking.

There were rich farms – like the previous one with its army of haystacks – and there were poor ones. This rough farmyard, with its single unwashed milking cow and milkmaid with chipped enamel bucket, shows a harsher aspect of farm life in the 1920s. Yet farming provided welcome work – occasional or regular – for men, women and children. When everything was done manually, 'hands' were always needed. When textile manufacturing declined after the First World War millhands were laid off and farmwork helped to fill the employment gap.

44 Horse power.

Good horses provided the power for farming whereby great landowners thrived and crofters advanced beyond subsistence farming on the strip of land behind their cottage (p.12) and their grazing rights on the Common Muir (p.29). If a crofter could get enough money, a feu and a good horse, he might yet become a farmer. Even in 1799 there were 100 ploughs in the parish, many of them 4-horse ploughs. Here in the local smithy may be seen farmhands' pride in their fine teams. The parlourmaid from a nearby house comes to share the picture and the pride.

45   Ploughs for sale.

Farming's traditional methods were turned to account at the turn of the century by a canny and industrious local blacksmith, Mr. Halley. This regiment of horse-drawn ploughs outside Baad's Smithy – below the bottom house in town, where a ford crossed the Ruthven – was for export to Canada, Australia, Europe – wherever good quality ploughs with an international reputation were needed. The busy smithy with its great furnaces threw out a blazing heat – a welcoming place in bad weather for passers-by and children to warm themselves and dry off while having a blether.

46 Railways – Auchterarder Station.

The coming of the railways was of dynamic importance in Auchterarder's history. Townsfolk who had never been further than Glasgow – unless emigrating – could travel great distances and yet not leave home forever. First, of course, they had to get used to the speed! *Thae trains they murder sic a lot / And rin past in a dint* (Tovani). Trains brought coal, coal brought power and power brought industry and work. No less than two stations were provided in 1856 by competing railways: Auchterarder Station by Scottish Central Railways and Crieff Junction – later Gleneagles – by Caledonian Railways (from 1923 the LMS). By ill judgement the town fathers required both stations to be built far from the town centre. It may not have semed so far to townsfolk who thought nothing of walking to Perth for a drink during the 'dry' years (p.8).

47 Railway Workers.

Railways brought employment. These Crieff Junction workers of all ages (one under age!) could look forward to a lifetime with the Caledonian and LMS Railways. The stations were immaculate and brilliant with flowers in the summer. Safety regulations were, perhaps, not very tight. In the 1880-1890s, as East Line and West Line express trains to London approached certain key crossings, bystanders were said to take keen interest in the race to see which arrived first. Signals were manual and children who made friends with kind signalmen were allowed to work them. The stations being inconveniently placed, Haldanes and other privileged persons could personally stop passing express trains to claim 'rights of passage'.

48   South Feus… weaving shed.

Until the railway brought industrial revolution handloom weaving was the main industry in the town – 500 handlooms in the parish in 1837. Behind many houses up the High Street were weaving sheds, where families shared the work. Young Mrs. Willie Dunlop and little Anne, sitting in Johnnie Moir's Park in 1932, have a distant view over the dry stone dyke, of a house built in 1797, with a single-storey shed for one or two handlooms. Andrew Faichney, its builder, a mason with six sons, augmented his income by weaving, sold through a middleman in Glasgow. When cottage looms were driven out by power looms the weaving shed became a two-room 'but and ben', still earning useful income by being let out to tenants.

49 The handloom weaver.

A rare picture of a handloom weaver at work. The whole family, from childhood, helped with the work, but the men set up the looms and kept them in order. It was exacting, noisy work – the clatter of the looms racketed up the High Street – but it represented independence and a few shillings a week. Home weavers lost their market when power looms took over. Many found employment in the mills, but Mr. Flockhart in Dunning carried on in the old way. Others emigrated; in one family seven brothers ended up in Toronto, Nova Scotia, Sacramento, Australia, New Zealand, Spain – and England.

50 Inside the mill.

In 1872 Hally moved to Ruthvenvale, near the source of water power and the railway station. Auchterarder's textile industry prospered. He produced high quality shirtings, wool angora – and miles of khaki and airforce blue during the war. Another manufacturer, Robert White, set up in Ruthvendale, specialising in silk taffeta, poplins. Then another – Young's. Employment – not least for women – expanded. In 1881 199 men and 390 women worked in the mills. Other industries grew: Mallis' Boot Factory, continuing local shoe-making traditions; Caws Dye Works – *We Dye to Live* – for the mills. With industry came professional services – two banks and a firm of solicitors, under William Young of Belvidere – pillar of the church and ardent Liberal. Auchterarder was becoming a manufacturing microcosm.

51   Hally railway rolling stock.

Increase from 25 looms in 1872 to 540 in 1892 was made possible by massive delivery of coal by the railways. A postcard of Hally's first rolling stock symbolises the railway contribution to industrial boom. In 1892 Hally's was producing 80,000 yards of shirtings a week, exported worldwide. Some millworkers lived in new terrace houses near the mills up Abbey Road, but many had far to walk – to Aberuthven or Castleton. A path across the fields past the Gas Works was a direct route to the Feus. But it was often convenient to walk home up Abbey Road, stopping off at the Railway Tavern for refreshment.

52 Provost William Hally.

This man led the Auchterarder industrial revolution (p.50). With several able sons he left his mark strongly on the town. First Provost of the new Burgh Town Council in 1894 he turned his ability and energy to civic problems: new underground drainage facilities (*very expensive; would a new scavenger be enough?*); increasing the water supply from Duchally (p.31); 100 new gas-lamp pillars in the streets; 1,000 yards of new pavement 6 feet wide; side streets lengthened for new housing (*"wynds' were no longer good enough*); better road surfaces for growing traffic. Times were changing in Auchterarder.

William Hally died aged 80, having had 16 children by his first wife and another when on her death he married again. Not surprisingly he was regarded with rare respect by not easily impressed townsfolk.

53 Builders and masons.

While industry grew there was a ceaseless demand for skilled tradesmen like these builders, stonemasons, carpenters, blacksmiths. Some were dry stone dykers, craftsmen who built the miles of uncemented walls which divided land between crofts and feus (p.42). Such expert work required long apprenticeship, but led to enviable self-employment, respected in the community. Men and boys like these built a large part of today's Auchterarder: public buildings, mills, shops and houses which by the First World War stretched far beyond the Lang Toon of the 19th century.

54 Domestic service.

The mills employed many women, but many more went into domestic service. There was a constant demand. No family of any substance before the First World War would be without a maid and if possible a cook. Houses like Cloan employed dozens of men and women, inside and out. The Cloan cook, seen here in 1880 with the table-maid, was a key member of a household in which precedence amongst servants was as strict as amongst the gentry. They worked all hours, according to their employers' requirements – rising before dawn to get the cleaning done before breakfast and to carry up water for baths. Their pay was not generous (e.g. Nannies £25 p.a.). But it brought some steady income into their families, especially valued when the mills began to lay workers off.

55 Auchterarder in arms.

These soldiers represent rugged Auchterarder men who served in the 6th Black Watch. Sam Lawson – on the right – is well remembered, first for surviving four years of war and then for his post-war years as local postman. It was an arduous life, catching the mail at six a.m. every morning as it was thrown off the train at Gleneagles Station and then travelling a round of twentysix miles on his bicycle with a heavy postbag to make deliveries. He kept good time and one special thing he never forgot – to stop at Mrs. Nicol's shop to buy sweeties for the bairns.

56 Cavalry manoeuvres, 1907.

Lord Haldane of Cloan, Secretary of State for War (p.28), keenly interested in army training and founder of the Territorial Army, organised army manoeuvres in the Ochils in 1907. About 1,000 men and 500 mounted troops camped in fields before Cloan. Territorial artillery, 18th Hussars, Seaforths, Scots Greys – as well as the 6th Black Watch, fully manned by Auchterarder lads – fought each other in mock battle over the hills. The townsfolk took a keen interest, but when English troops tried to elicit information about the whereabouts of Scottish units they were met with stony silence.

57   The Red Cross gets started.

Miss Haldane (p.26) took a leading part in developing the British Red Cross and V.A.D. services which proved their worth in the First World War. To promote knowledge of their work she organised displays of nursing alongside army manoeuvres at Cloan. Here, in 1911, volunteers (in their impractical uniforms) care for a cadet under the admiring eyes of Lord Haldane and guests. Five years later, in real life, the scene was re-enacted when the boy lost an eye in the Battle of the Somme – fortunate not to be one of the 20,000 who died that day.

58 Boy Scouts.

Lord Baden Powell was amongst the distinguished visitors to the Haldanes of Cloan. It was remarkable how many visitors, one way or another, were encouraged to make a contribution to the town: the Archbishop of Canturbury preached at Episcopalian St. Kessog's Church; Andrew Carnegie supported the Library; Lord Kelvin supervised the first electricity power from Cloan Dam. So too the town had one of the earliest Boy Scout troops, inspired by Baden Powell. Here they are outside the school, rehearsing life-saving exercises which their fathers used in real life in France.

59   The death of a soldier.

In 1912, before the carnage of the First World War made soldiers' deaths familiar – 84 names on the Auchterarder War Memorial – one young lance corporal of the Scottish Horse, James Meldrum, died of illness and was buried with honours befitting a general. *The farming interest was represented by no less than 25 gigs'; pipers were sent by Lord Tullibardine. As a local poet wrote: Slowly the cortege wended its way to the tomb / Attended by friends, comrades, playmates, chums / The 'Flowers of the Forest' and 'The Land of the Leal' / Sounded sweetly though weirdly as they bore him along…*

60 Guarding Kincardine Viaduct.

The Kincardine Viaduct carried over Kindardine Castle estate the railway which transformed Auchterarder life. It was a fine bit of engineering and an essential wartime route for men and materials. Local recruits of the 6th Black Watch guarded it from 1914 to 1918. One carried the gun. One played the flute. In relaxed moments they probably sang the popular song:

O why did I join the 6th Black Watch?
O why did I join the army?
O why did I join the 6th Black Watch?
I think I must have been barmy!

During the First World War 492 Auchterarder men, out of a population of about 2,500, served with the colours – 179 in the Black Watch.

61   Nurses and patients.

Strathallan Castle was the seat of the Viscounts Strathallan from 1225 – a branch of the Drummond family, of whom three were attainted as Jacobites. In 1910 the family sold the estate to Sir James Roberts and during the First World War the Castle with its fine gardens was used as a Red Cross convalescent hospital for wounded soldiers. After the rigours of the trenches it must have been a pleasant refuge. Scottish troops enjoyed teaching reels to their nurses. In the Second World War Strathallan Castle was a school for girls evacuated from Glasgow.

62 Armistice Day 1918.

On 11 November 1918, after four years of brutal warfare, Auchterarder celebrated the Armistice. The official ceremonies had been in Aytoun Hall, whence this stream of townsfolk was marching up Townhead for further celebration in the public park. They were joined by VAD nurses from Strathallan Castle's Convalescent Hospital. A cheerful cap is raised to the camera in greeting and flags have been hoisted. Eighty-four names of Auchterarder men killed in action were recorded on the War Memorial.

63 The next generation.

The Sunday School picnic in 1920 is a good opportunity to glimpse the next generation enjoying the fine summer weather and familiar pleasures. *It was a lovely afternoon / The sun was shining brightly doon / As we gaed cheerin' doon the toun / And took our way to braw Cloan Den.* Teachers and older girls wore hats, of course, and most boys wore collars and ties. Is there a slackening of propriety in the two men not wearing jackets? Virtually all children went to one of the Sunday Schools and most belonged to the Band of Hope – swearing weekly to 'abstain from all intoxicating liquors and… to try to induce others to do likewise'. There was a lot of innocent optimism around.

64 Growing up.

In 1929 the Third Year Form posed on the steps of Auchterarder School, with science master Albert Wilson. A few went on to Perth Academy or Morrisons in Crieff, but in these years of the Depression most were soon looking for work. It was not foreseen that they would grow up just in time for a war which changed their lives. All the boys and several girls joined the forces. Isa Fyffe married a Polish soldier posted to the area. Madge Cairns did war service as a railway porter at Gleneagles Station. Some became professionals – like Betty Gamble, a teacher – and Willie MacNaughton, a lawyer. The Police Sergeant's son went to fight in Burma and ended up a bank manager in India. They were to scatter far and wide. But Willie Kemp, a journalist, never lost touch and wrote vividly of the town he knew so well.

65 Girl Guides.

The Girl Guides were active and proud in their military style uniforms. The Boy Scouts started in 1908 but the Guides – originally 'Scouts' – followed suit in 1910. This local troop in the 1930s, with their much-loved Captain Nan Brownlee and Lieutenant Agnes Smith, took part in the Perth Music Festival, winning both 1st and 2nd prizes in the Scottish Country Dancing Competition. Music still played a large part in local life. The Rev. Jacque would have been pleased (p. 23). One girl, Jan White, was long the organist in Barony Church, after service in the Wrens. Many others, like Nan Cairns and Dollie Bayne, served in the forces. Martha Soutar, after serving with the WAAFs on an American base, gave lifetime service to the railways at Gleneagles Station. For some the war opened new doors: Lieutenant Agnes Smith married a teaplanter in India; Janet Roy married a Canadian serviceman and emigrated with him.

66 The Coal Bore.

Children in Auchterarder during all these years found exciting places to play, like the Coal Bore, down by the Ruthven. In the last century attempts had been made to open a coal mine. Coal from Fife was costly and a local source would have been valuable, but there proved to be not enough to exploit. All that was left was a shallow hole between the Gelly Burn and the great, grey prehistoric Granny Stane. Filled with water the hole proved a fine place for a splash. There were seats for the elderly, behind which swimmers could change with modesty.

67 The Club House, Auchterarder Golf Course.

In 1892 nine Auchterarder gentlemen met at the Queen's Hotel and decided to apply to the Common Muir Commissioners (p.29) for the right to build a nine-hole golf course over the fields of Clashintock, North Second Hoew, Geil's Quarry and Martin's Park. The first club house was a corrugated iron roofed shed. Then from 1913 to 1973 this unpretentious building served golfers' needs. The course itself was precious; rolling was done by horses shod with soft leather boots rather than iron horse shoes. Greenkeepers honoured grazing rights over the Common Muir by building stiles over dividing walls. A problem in this strictly Presbyterian township was playing on Sunday; not until servicemen were allowed to play during the war was the Sabbath breached. In 1948 the Town Council sanctioned Sunday play in the afternoon. (Picture by courtesy of Auchterarder Golf Club.)

68   Golf in Auchterarder.

Golf at its best requires good greens, fine fairways and scenery. This picture of Auchterarder's course suggests the quality of enjoyment golfers found on the old Common Muir. It could become an obsession. Three hundred years previously it was recounted of the marriage of local hero the Marquis of Montrose: *Having finished his match... the previous day and greeted his bride to be... he was married on 10th November 1629, but scarcely had the minstrels ceased to serenade them when we find Montrose at his clubs and balls again...* (Picture by courtesy of Auchterarder Golf Club.)

69 Bowling Green.

Sport of all kinds was popular in Auchterarder before and after the First World War. Golf was, of course, plentiful and obsessional; the County had clubs for Ladies, Artisans, Licensed Victuallers, etc. Clubs for Quoits, Cycling, Motoring, Ice Hockey, Riding were all listed in the Annual Register. In season there were angling, curling and shooting. Tennis courts, bowling greens and a cricket field were accommodated in the North Crofts and much used. No less than three football clubs competed in local and even national leagues. Below: Bowling was hotly contested with neighbouring communities on this favourite Green. Auchterarder's bowling elite in 1909 won the Whitelaw Cup. There was no distinction between managers, landowners and artisans on the bowling green. Here was a cross section of Auchterarder male society.

70   Football.

Football in Auchterarder as everywhere in Scotland was 'the beautiful game'. When it was less easy than now to get to Perth to see St. Johnstone in county matches, there were three or four active teams in the town. Proudest of all were Thistle, who in 1903 even played Rangers at Ibrox! (They lost.) Many young footballers never came back from the war – but there was a new start with juvenile teams like the up and coming Victoria Football Club in 1925. David McLeod has the ball between his feet.

71 Mixed Hockey!

Golf, bowls, curling, tennis… every sort of sport for men or women was available and ardently played in the Lang Toon. But who would expect to find here hockey played at the turn of the century by a mixed team of men and women? Of course mixed doubles in tennis and even golf were pleasant social pastimes, but hockey was serious, physical, hard-hitting competitive sport. Minds were more liberated than we credit!

72 'Greetings from Auchterarder'.

In 1914 building stopped on a half finished Gleneagles Hotel. In 1919 the LMS Railway hastened to make up for lost time. They succeeded beyond expectation. By 1924 the hotel felt able to call itself *the Palace in the Glens… the Playground of the Gods… Britain's Distinguished Resort for Fashionable Recreation*. The attractions of Auchterarder and surrounding countryside were included in the advertising. A small branch railway brought guests almost to the door, but some young debs flew in with their boy friends. Indian Maharajas, European princes and American film stars were common visitors. Henry Hall's dance band broadcast from here. It was a roaring success. Auchterarder benefited from the glamour and prosperity of this new neighbour. Objection only came from the Laird of Glen Eagles, the Haldane seat. He fought a doughty albeit unsuccessful battle to prevent usurpation of his home's dinstinguished name.

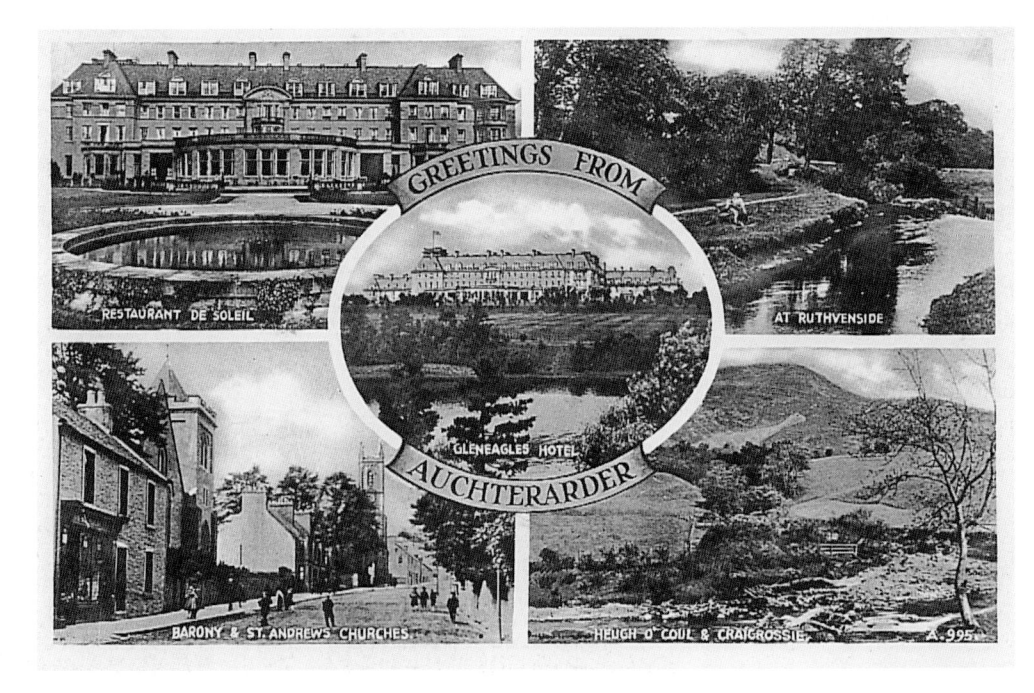

73 'Gleneagles Hospital'.

During the Second World War there was no time for luxury hotels. Gleneagles Hotel became a hospital. Previously exclusive bedrooms costing £1,000 a month became wards for wounded servicemen – seven or more to a room. Patients were of all nationalities; amongst the first came Polish sailors, whose destroyer sank at Narvik in 1940. Convalescence included local sightseeing and hospitality by friendly local families, who brought marmalade and homemade gingerbread, despite rationing. It was not a bad billet for men who had been through hell.

74 Patients at Gleneagles.

Nurses, patients and doctors formed congenial friendships. A fully-equipped hospital train brought the wounded to Gleneagles Station. The Drawing Room was for convalescents, the Glendevon suite for skin treatment. One surgical ward had 62 beds. One day, in less than two hours, a hundred patients were admitted after a ship was torpedoed. They carried little more than their waterproof bracelets with name and number. The old swimming pool was a mortuary.

75 The war is over!

The shining faces in this picture of Rossie Place on VJ night – August 1945 – tell their own story. Many servicemen from Auchterarder had served with the Chindits in the Burmese war and victory over Japan brought even more relief to their families than the victory in Europe. Many men – and women too – were really coming home at last, although some were not actually demobbed until 1947. New Council house areas like Rossie Place had developed before and during the war. They already enjoyed a strong community atmosphere, rather like the old wynds off the High Street in earlier generations. The party went on all night.

76 'Heartiest greetings from Auchterarder'.

This old postcard from before the First World War reflects abiding memories of Auchterarder: The Auld House of Gask (p.39), Coul Falls (p.28), warmth of friendship, and tenacity of principle:

Come wi' me across the dell
To yon lang toon.
On yonder brae wi' gentle swell
Its crest doth croon.
Famed Auchterarder for disputes
Independent men and lang law suits.

(Scottish Herald, November 1902.)